# Guitar Method

**Ron Manus**
**Morty Manus**

## Get Down to BASIX™!

BASIX™ is all you need to take off with your instrument. Alfred has worked hard to help you begin learning today with our easy-to-use, comprehensive series. It won't frustrate you by moving too fast, or let you get bored by moving too slow! You'll notice pics of many great performers; we added those to fire your imagination and help you stay focused on becoming a star yourself! To top it off, you can put what you learn to work when you play along with the companion CD. Set your sights high by beginning with BASIX™... the series that will get you there!

Cover photos: Martin Guitar Company (Acoustic);
Fender Musical Instruments, Scottsdale, Arizona (Electric)

# Contents

***Eric Clapton*** *is one of rock's most influential guitarists. His passion for American blues music has been evident in Clapton's playing since his earliest recordings with John Mayall's Bluesbreakers and The Yardbirds. He has gone on to sell millions of records, and continues to inspire generations of musicians.*

# What You Should Know Before Starting this Book

If you have completed Books 1 and 2 of Basix™ Guitar Method, you will know the following about playing the guitar:

All the notes in the 1st position including sharps and flats:

The basic rhythms, including:

WHOLE NOTES     HALF NOTES     QUARTER NOTES     EIGHTH NOTES     DOTTED QUAR and EIGHTH N•

TIE

DOTTED HALF NOTE

WHOLE REST     HALF REST     QUARTER REST     EIGHTH REST

You should also know the following chords: F minor in its three-string form, C G G7, D7 and D minor in their string forms, A minor in its five-string form and E7 in its six-string form. These will be reviewed where approp

And you should understand such miscellaneous (but important) information as pickups, tempo signs (Andante, Moderato, Allegro), bass/chord accompaniments, dynamics (*p mf f ff*), crescendo ( ——— and diminuendo ( ——————— ), key signatures in C (no sharps or flats), G (one sharp), and F (one fla the meaning of *D.C.* (*da capo,* go back to the beginning), *D.S. al fine* (*dal segno,* go back to the sign 𝄋 play through to the word *fine*), 1st and 2nd endings and syncopation.

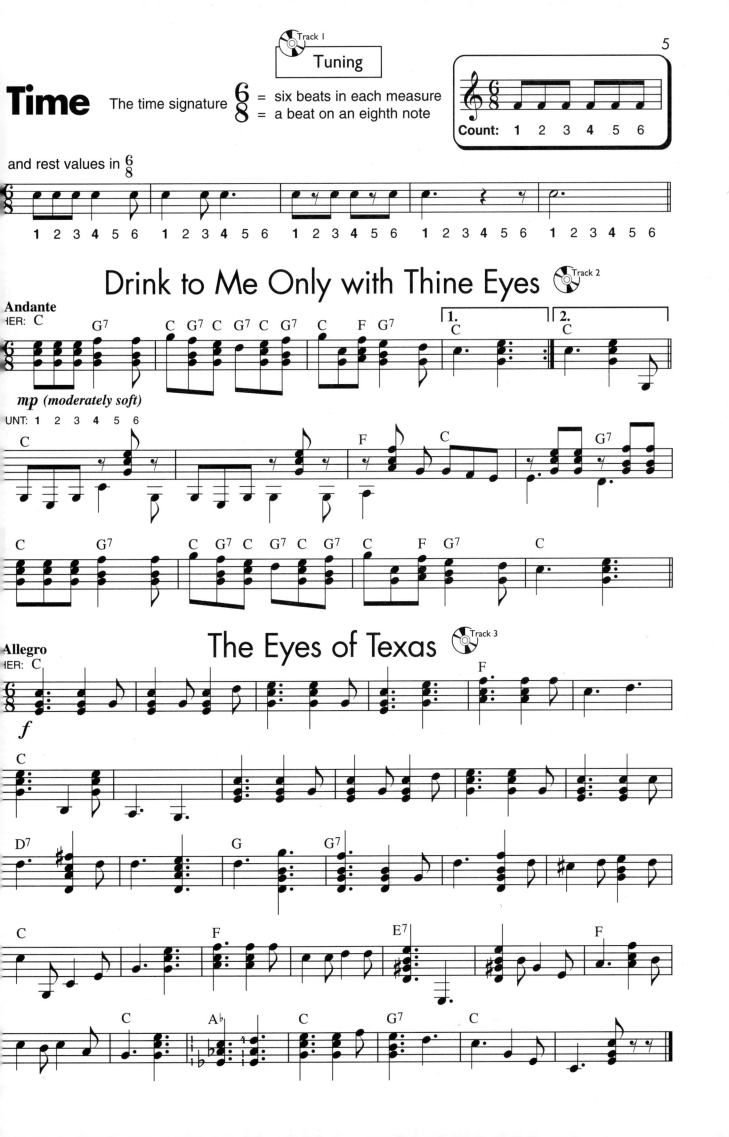

# For He's a Jolly Good Fellow
Track 4

*Go back to the s
and play to the

# Funiculi, Funicula
Track 5

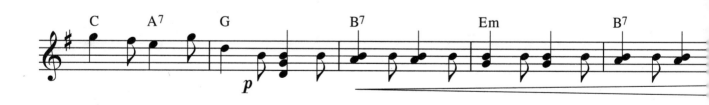

# The Irish Washerwoman

Track 6

Irish Folk Tune

**Allegro**

TEACHER:

KEEP 3rd FINGER DOWN

*One of the most popular bands to emerge during the mid-1990s, hailing from Ireland, the Cranberries play compelling pop-tunes upon which lead-singer **Delores O'Riordan's** hypnotic vocals soar.*

# Bass-Chord Accompaniment: Key of G

The three principal chords in the key of G are G, C, D7:

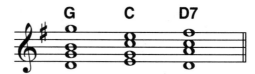

**THE THREE PRINCIPAL CHORDS WITH THE ROOT\* BASS.**

## Bass–Chord–Chord–Chord   Track 7

## Bass–Chord–Bass–Chord   Track 8

## Bass–Chord Variation   Track 9

\*The root of a chord is the note that names it. For example, the root of a G chord is the note G; the root of a D7 chord is D an

# Oh! Susanna

(Duet)

Stephen Foster

# The Key of D Major

The key signature of two sharps indicates the key of D major. All F's are played as F♯ and all C's are played C♯ unless otherwise indicated by a natural sign. To play the two-octave D major scale, you'll need two new notes on the 1st string, high C♯ (1st string, 9th fret) and high D (1st string, 10th fret).

When learning the two-octave D major scale below, follow the fingering carefully. Like all scales, this one should be practiced daily.

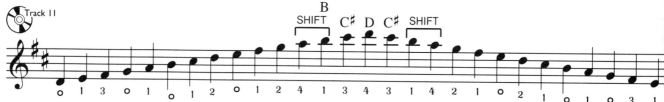

## The Three Principal Chords in D with Bass Notes

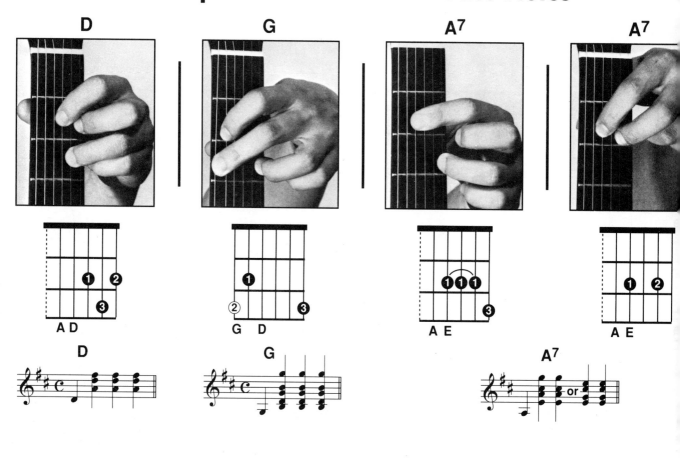

## Accompaniment in D Major

# Two Etudes in D  Track 13

e student should learn both the melody and the accompanying chords of this Christmas favorite.

**Majestically**

# Joy to the World  Track 14

# Marines Hymn

(Duet)

# ne Dotted 8th &
# 6th Note Rhythm

8th notes, dotted 8ths and 16ths are played two to each beat.  But unlike 8th notes (which are played
nly) dotted 8ths and 16ths are played unevenly:  long, short, long, short.

npare the following:

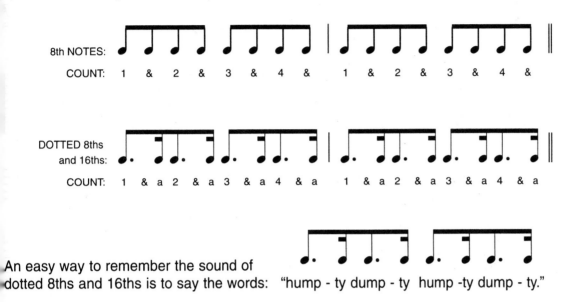

8th NOTES:

COUNT:  1  &  2  &  3  &  4  &     1  &  2  &  3  &  4  &

DOTTED 8ths
and 16ths:

COUNT:  1  &  a  2  &  a  3  &  a  4  &  a     1  &  a  2  &  a  3  &  a  4  &  a

An easy way to remember the sound of
dotted 8ths and 16ths is to say the words:   "hump - ty dump - ty  hump -ty dump - ty."

dotted 8th and 16th note rhythm is very common in all kinds of music, but especially classical, folk, coun-
and blues.  Here are examples of each to practice.

## Toreador Song (from *Carmen*) 🄯 Track 16

Geo. Bizet

Student to play melody and chords.

# Straight Jig

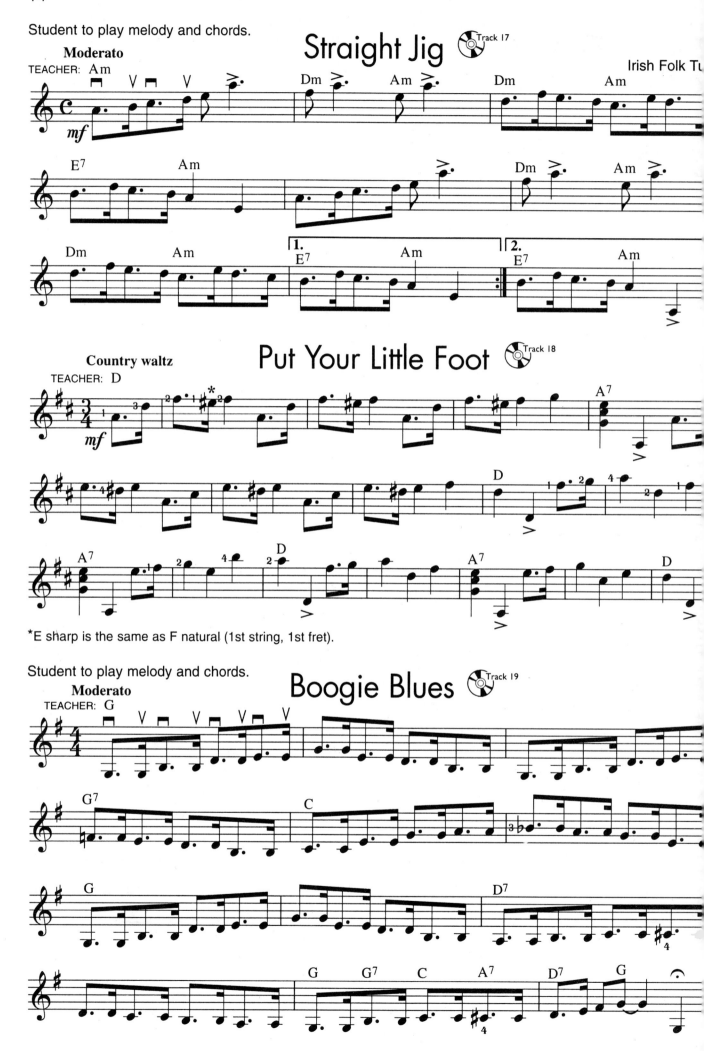

Track 17

Irish Folk Tune

*E sharp is the same as F natural (1st string, 1st fret).

Student to play melody and chords.

dotted 8th and 16th note rhythm can be combined with bass-chord style to create a type of accompani-
t called the "shuffle beat." Keep in mind the "hump-ty dump-ty" rhythm of the accompaniment and use
n- and up-picking to accomplish it.

# Careless Love
## (Duet)

Track 20

**Moderate shuffle beat**

Traditional Blues

means to repeat previous measure.

# Alternating Bass Notes

An alternating bass note is any note except the root of the chord (usually the 5th). Alternate bass notes are used to enrich the accompaniment when the harmony remains the same for several consecutive measures

The accompaniment is good:

But this is better:

## Alternating Bass Notes in the Key of C

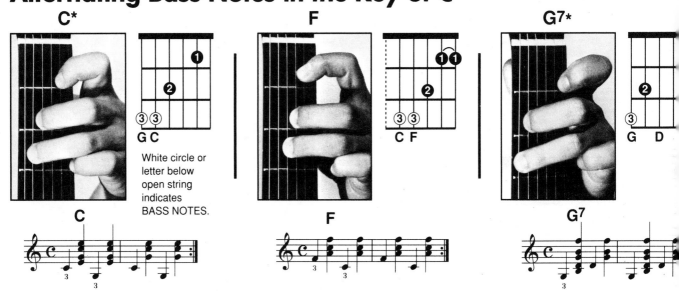

White circle or letter below open string indicates BASS NOTES.

## Accompaniment in C Major  Track 21

*Here are complete forms of the C and G7 chords. If the stretches can be handled, their use is preferred when playing accompaniment. Finger the complete chord at the beginning of the measure and hold it until the chord changes.

# I Ride an Old Paint*

Track 22

(Duet)

paint is a horse with a smear of color.

ll off means: Do not pick the 2nd note. Pull the 2nd finger off the string so that the open G note sounds.

# Alternating Bass Notes in the Key of G

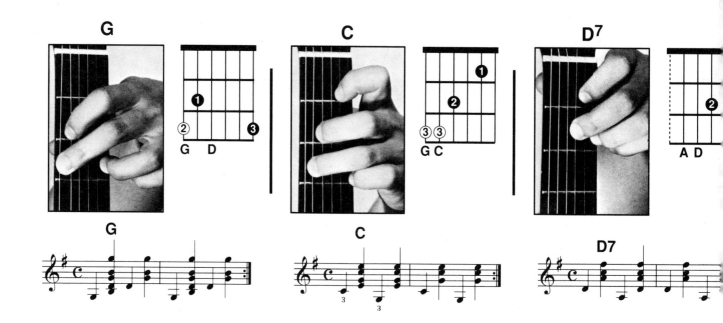

## Accompaniment in G Major

# Hand Me Down My Walking Cane

(Duet)

# Introducing Triplets

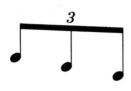

When three notes are grouped together with the figure "3" above or below the notes, the group is called a TRIPLET. The three notes then have the same value as is ordinarily given to two of the notes. In 3/4 or 4/4 times, two eighth notes get one count, so an eighth note TRIPLET will also get one count.

Track 25

In the following exercise play the three notes of each triplet on one count.

## Triumphal March (from *Aida*)  Track 26

Giuseppe V

**Maestoso**
(Majestically)

*\*D.C.* means go back to the beginning. *D.C. al Fine* means go back to the beginning and play to the end (*Fine*).

# Beautiful Dreamer  Track 27

Stephen Foster

## Sweet Genevieve Track 28

**PLAY:** G7  C  /  F  G7  /  /  G7  /  /  C  /  /

SING: Oh, Gen - e - vieve, sweet Gen - e - vieve, The days may come, the days may go, But

C  /  /  F  /  /  C  /  /  G7  C

still the hands of mem - 'ry weave the bliss - ful dreams of long a - go.

*Since the 1960s, **Neil Young** has been a rock 'n' roll chameleon, always exploring new styles, often incorporating obscure styles years before they became popular. He is one of popular music's greatest pioneers.*

Photo: © Ken Settle

# Key of E Minor

E minor and G Major are relative keys, they both have the key signature of one sharp (F♯.) Like the A minor scale, the E minor scale is built on the 6th tone of the relative (G) major.

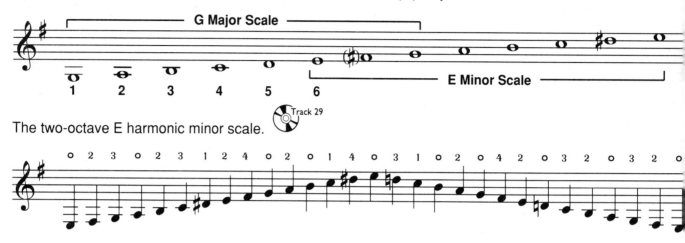

The two-octave E harmonic minor scale.

## The Three Principal Chords in the Key of E Minor

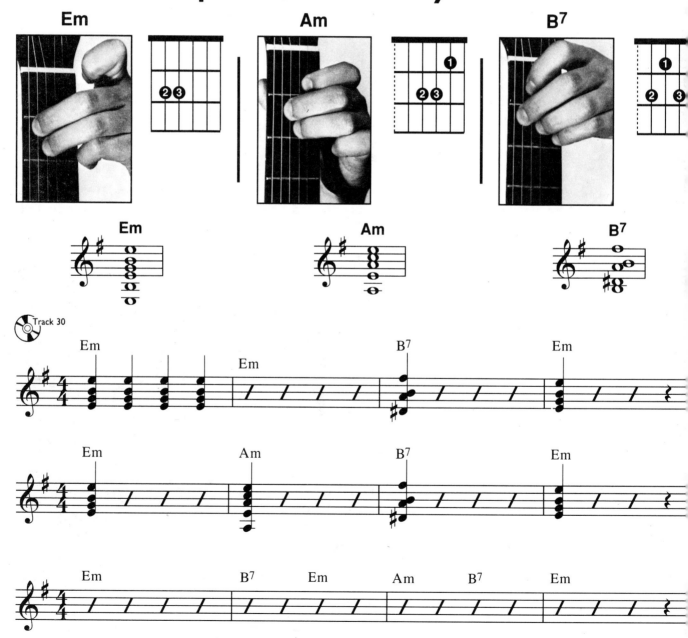

# Etude in E Minor

Track 31

# Joshua Fit the Battle

Track 32

Gospel Tune

**Moderately, with a beat**

rn the melody and chords.

TEACHER: Em

Josh - ua  fit  the  bat - tle  of___  Jer - i - cho,___  Jer - i - cho,___

Jer - i - cho;___  Josh - ua  fit  the  bat - tle  of___  Jer - i  cho___  and the

walls  came  tum - blin'  down. (That  morn - in')___  down.

You  may  talk  a - bout  your  King  of  Gid - e - on,  You  may

talk  a - bout  your  man  of  Saul,  But there's  none  like  good  old

*D.C. al Fine**

Josh - u - a___  at the  bat - tle  of  Jer - i - cho.

member to play from the beginning.  Skip the 1st ending and end with the 2nd ending.

# Alternating Bass Notes in the Key of F

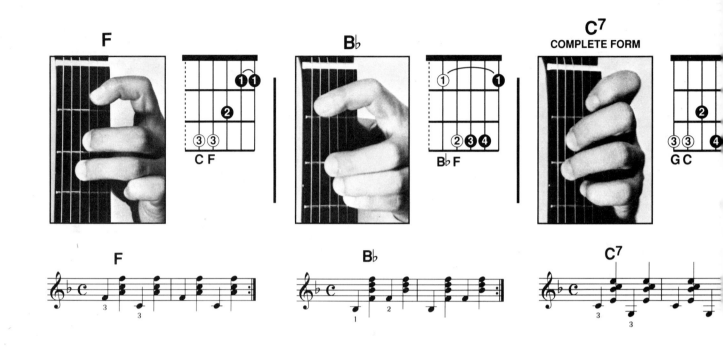

## Accompaniment in F Major

Track 33

# Oh, My Darling Clementine

(Duet)

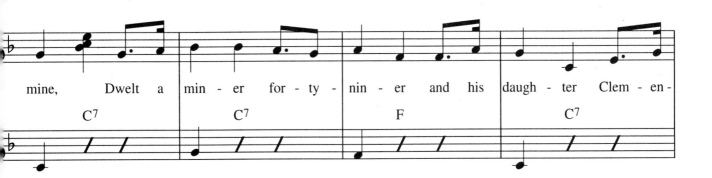

In a cav - ern in a can - yon ex - ca - vat - ing for a

mine, Dwelt a min - er for - ty - nin - er and his daugh - ter Clem - en -

tine. Oh my dar - ling, oh my dar - ling, oh my dar - ling Clem - en -

tine; You are lost and gone for - ev - er, dread - ful sor - ry, Clem - en - tine.

# Shave and a Haircut

**Briskly**

Before attempting this famous march by John Philip Sousa, you may want to review the discussion of 6/8 t
on page 5.

# The Liberty Bell
## (Duet)

John Philip So

**Brisk march tempo**

marcato accent (∧ or ∨) is a stressed accent.

# Alexander's Ragtime Band

Solo or Duet

Track 37

Irving B[...]

# Sixteenth Notes

Sixteenth notes are black notes with two flags added to the stems  or

Generally when two or more sixteenth notes are played, they are joined with two beams:

Sixteenth notes are played four to a beat, twice as fast as eighth notes and four times as fast as quarter no
Use alternate picking when playing sixteenth notes.

**4 quarter notes = 8 eighth notes = 16 sixteenth notes**

**In 2/4 time**

**In 3/4 time**

## Mixin' It Up  Track 38

*Fine*

*D.C. al Fi*

The pattern of an eighth note followed by two sixteenth notes is very common. The following song illustrates it. Watch the picking carefully.

## The Happy Sailor

The rhythm of two sixteenth notes followed by an eighth note is also fairly common. Again, watch your picking carefully.

## Variations on a Square Dance Tune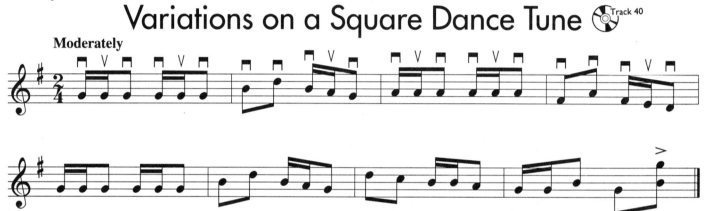

*Dwight Yoakum* *is one of the few country artists to successfully cross over to rock. Starting in the 1980s, Yoakum acquired a devout following loyal to his brand of rootsy, blues-influenced music.*

Photo: © Ken Settle

# Introducing Arpeggios

When the notes of a chord ♪ are played in succession ♪ it is an ARPEGGIO.

## East Side, West Side · Track 41

## The Man on the Flying Trapeze · Track 42

# Scarborough Fair
### (Duet)

Track 43

This beautiful English folk song was a big hit for Simon and Garfunkel in the '60s. It is arranged here as a duet, and the student should learn both parts. Keep the arpeggios flowing smoothly in the second part with fingers held down as long as possible.

# The Doo-Wop Ballad

In the 1950s a style of rock and roll ballad called "doo-wop" became very popular. This type of song featured many long held notes sung over an accompaniment of triplets, played either as chords or arpeggios. Here are a few samples of each.

**Key of C** (Chords)

The same chords played as arpeggios:

Important: Hold fingers down for the above arpeggios as long as possible

**Key of G** (Chords)

Arpeggios:

**Key of C Chords, with bass notes**

**Key of C, with variations**

**Key of G Chords, with bass notes**

**Key of G, with variations**

Here is a song written in '50s "doo-wop" style. Learn the melody and arpeggio-style accompaniment.

# My Angel Baby

Track 50

# The Key of A Major

The key signature of three sharps indicates the key of A major. All F's are played as F♯, all C's are played as C♯, and all G's are played as G♯ unless otherwise indicated by a natural sign.

When learning the two-octave A major scale below, follow the fingering carefully. Like all scales, this one should be practiced daily.

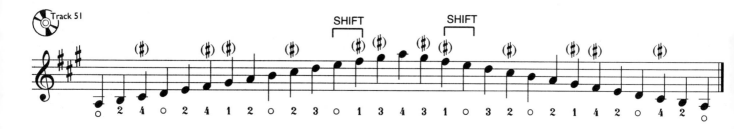

## The Three Principal Chords in A with Bass Notes

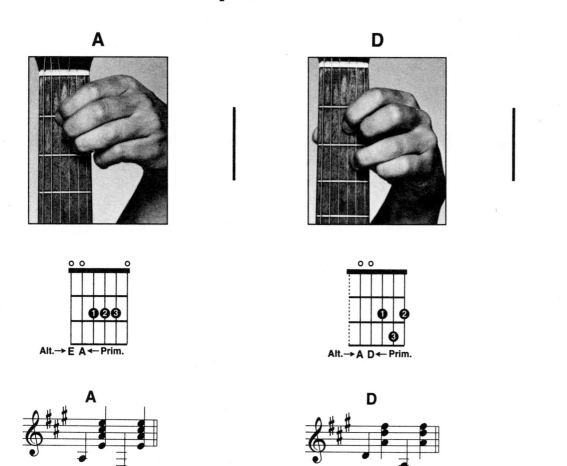

| A | D | E7 |
|---|---|---|
| Alt.→ E  A ←Prim. | Alt.→ A  D ←Prim. | Prim.→ E  B ←Alt. |

# Accompaniments in A Major
Track 52

## Arpeggio Style

Photo: © Ken Settle

*Often referred to as "the guitar player's guitar player,"* **Joe Satriani** *has been a mentor to the likes of Steve Vai and Metallica's Kirk Hammett. He is quietly one of the most respected guitarists of the 1980s and 1990s.*

# Scale Etude in A Major  Track 53

# Arpeggio Etude  Track 54

HOLD FINGERS IN PLACE AS LONG AS POSSIBLE

# Hard, Ain't It Hard

Track 55

Traditional

**Bright country tempo**

It's hard, and it's hard, ain't it hard to

love one that nev - er did love you. And it's

hard, ain't it hard, yes, it's hard, dear Lord, to

love one who nev - er could be true.

# Hail, Hail, The Gang's All Here

Track 56

Words: Anon.

Music: Sir Arthur Sullivan

**Like a march, in 2 (♩. = 1 beat)**

Hail, hail, the gang's all here;

What the heck do we care? What the heck do we care?

Hail, hail, the gang's all here;

What the heck do we care now?

# Sixteenth Note Studies in A Major  Track 57

Track 58